The Tamarindo Puppy

and Other Poems

by Charlotte Pomerantz

pictures by Byron Barton

 Greenwillow Books, New York

Library of Congress Cataloging in Publication Data   Pomerantz, Charlotte. The Tamarindo puppy and other poems. Summary: An illustrated collection of 13 poems which contain a sprinkling of Spanish. [1. American poetry] I. Barton, Byron. II. Title.   PS3566.0538T3   811'.5'4   79-16584   ISBN 0-688-80251-6   ISBN 0-688-84251-8 lib. bdg.

FOR AMELIA OCASIO AND PEDRO SANTANA RONDA

CONTENTS

THE TAMARINDO PUPPY

The Tamarindo puppy
Is a very nice puppy
Is a muy lindo puppy
Whom we visit every day.

But the Tamarindo puppy,
When we went there Monday morning,
The Tamarindo puppy
Aw
Had gone away.

What happened to the puppy,
The Tamarindo puppy,
Lindo, lindo puppy,
Whom we saw every day?

Did somebody see him
And say, "Oh, how darling!"
Did somebody see him
And say, "Ay, qué lindo!"
Did somebody see him
And take him home to play?

Does he like his new home,
The Tamarindo puppy?
Does he like his new friends,
Muy lejos, far away?

Or does he miss the breeze
In the Tamarindo trees
And his friends who came to visit him
Every single day?

FIRE HOUSE

Parque de bombas—boom boo.
Parque de vacas—moo moo.
Parque de perros—bow wow.
Parque de gatos—meow meow.

Parque de fire engines pumping,
Parque de bombas, bombas, boo.
Parque de vacas, vacas, vacas,
Parque de cows and moo, moo, moo.
Parque de perros, perros, perros,
Parque de dogs and bow wow wow.
Parque de gatos, gatos, gatos,
Parque de cats and meow, meow, meow.

Parque de bombas—boom boo.
Parque de vacas—moo moo.
Parque de perros—bow wow.
Parque de gatos—meow meow.

YOU—TU

You are you.
Not me,
But you.
Look in the mirror
Peek-a-boo
The face that you see
Isn't me—
It's you.

Tú eres tú.
No yo,
Pero tú.
Mira al espejo
Peek-a-boo
La cara que miras
No soy yo—
Eres tú.

MY FAT CAT

My fat cat
snoozing in the hay
zz zz zz zz
dreaming of the little mouse
the chummy mouse
the yummy mouse
the kind that fills-your-tummy mouse
who
     got
         away.

Gato mío, gato gordo
snoozing in the hay
zz zz zz zz
dreaming of the little mouse
ratoncito pequeñito
amiguito
sabrosito
zz zz zz zz
who
     got
         away.

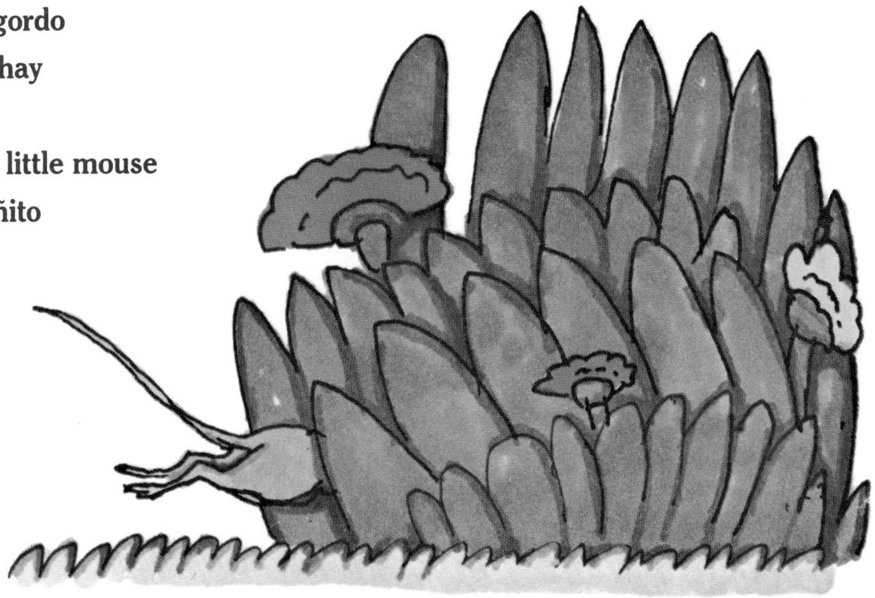

CACHITA

Cachita
is a little dog
who sleeps
at the foot
of my bed.
She always sleeps
at the foot
of my camita
except
when she sleeps
close by my cabecita,
close by my little head
at the head
of my bed.
Otherwise,
my little dog Cachita
sleeps at my feet
at the foot
of my camita.

A LITTLE LULLABY
TO BE READ A LITTLE BIT OUT LOUD

Take your bottle,
Little bottle.
Take your little botellita.
Little, little,
Pequeñita.
Botellita
Pequeñita.
Drink the little
Little milk.
Leche, leche,
Mmm, lechita.
Nice and warm,
Mmm, tibiecita.
Lechecita
Tibiecita.

Sleep now in your little bed.
Sleep awhile in your camita,
In your little camitita.
Little, little, little bed.

THE TEA PARTY

Pucho, put the kettle on.
We'll all have tea.
Cucho, take it off again.
Where can *Pucho* be?

Cucho, put the kettle on.
Pucho, take it off again.
Ay ay ay, muchacho,
Where can *Cucho* be?

Will *someone* put the kettle on?
Will *someone* take the kettle off?
Ay ay ay, muchacho,
There's no one here but me!

Caramba, Cucho-Pucho!
Caramba, Pucho-Cucho!
I will put the kettle on
And have some tea.

Here comes naughty Pucho.
Here comes naughty Cucho.
Both of them are yelling,
Mamma, give us tea!

Sorry, Cucho-Pucho.
Lo siento, Pucho-Cucho.
Lo siento mucho, mucho.
This tea is just for me.

MY MAMI TAKES ME TO THE BAKERY

Let's buy pan de agua, daughter.
Pan is bread and agua, water.
Good fresh bread of flour and water.
Good fresh pan de agua, daughter.

Inside the panadería,
There's the hot sweet smell of pan.
Good day, says the plump panadero.
(The baker's a very nice man.)

How many loaves, Señora, he asks:
Uno…dos?
Dos? Sí, sí.
Two, por favor, says my mami.
Two loaves for my daughter and me.

HUGS AND KISSES

Mami, how long will you be away?

      I'll be gone for a month, María.

Then give me a kiss for every day,
For every day that you are away.

      That's thirty small kisses, María.
      Treinta besitos, one for each day.
      One for each day that I am away.
      Treinta besitos, María.

Now give me a hug for every day,
For every day that you are away.

      That's thirty big hugs, María.
      Treinta abrazos, one for each day.
      One for each day that I am away.
      Treinta abrazos, María.

Now give me a doll for every day,
For every day that you are away.

      That's thirty dollies, María.
      Treinta muñecas, one for each day.
      One for each day that I am away.
      No, indeed, María.

MARISOL

My friend's name is Marisol.

Mar is the sea.

Sol is the sun.

I dream, I dream of Marisol.

Sueño del mar,

De Mar y sol,

When the golden day is done.

THE FOUR BROTHERS

Fito is a farmer and he lives in Aguadilla.
Chito is a teacher and he lives in Guayanilla.
Tito is a poet and he lives in a tree.
But Lalito is a baby and he lives with me.

Fito married Fita and they had a son Fitito.
Chito married Chita and they had a son Chitito.
Tito still writes poetry and lives in a tree.
But Lalito is a little boy and lives with me.

When Fitito grew up, he got married to Fitita.
When Chitito grew up, he got married to Chitita.
When Tito got old, he came down from the tree.
And Lalito, my Lalito, no longer lives with me.

Now Lalito is a plumber and he lives in Aibonito,
With Lalita, who's an engineer and works in Naranjito,
And they have a little son, very little, muy chiquito,
And they named him—did you guess it?—Willy.

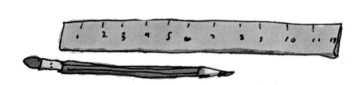

Fito

Chito

Tito

Lalito

27

MARI ROSA AND THE BUTTERFLY

Mariposa, butterfly,
Mariposa, fluttering by,
Why oh why oh why can't I
Be a Mariposa?

Mari Rosa, dancing by,
Dancing, prancing, braids tossed high.
Why oh why oh why can't I
Be a Mari Rosa?

NADA

Nada is nothing.
Nothing at all.
Trip on a nada,
You never will fall.
Is the room empty?
Then nada is there.
Muchísima nada
Is everywhere.
So if you have nada,
Do not be sad.
Always remember
what you never had—
nada.